First World War
and Army of Occupation
War Diary
France, Belgium and Germany

2 DIVISION
3 Light Brigade
Rifle Brigade (The Prince Consort's Own)
51 Battalion
28 March 1919 - 2 November 1919

WO95/1374/10

The Naval & Military Press Ltd
www.nmarchive.com
Published in association with The National Archives

Published by

The Naval & Military Press Ltd

Unit 10 Ridgewood Industrial Park,

Uckfield, East Sussex,

TN22 5QE England

Tel: +44 (0) 1825 749494

www.naval-military-press.com

www.nmarchive.com

This diary has been reprinted in facsimile from the original. Any imperfections are inevitably reproduced and the quality may fall short of modern type and cartographic standards.

© **Crown Copyright**
Images reproduced by permission of The National Archives, London, England, 2015.

Contents

Document type	Place/Title	Date From	Date To
Heading	WO95/1374/10		
Heading	2 Division 3 Light Brigade 51 Bn Rifle Brigade 1919 Mar 1919 Oct		
War Diary	Stommeln	28/03/1919	07/04/1919
War Diary	Bedburg	08/04/1919	17/06/1919
War Diary	Glessen	18/06/1919	18/06/1919
War Diary	Coln Nippes	19/06/1919	28/06/1919
War Diary	Poulheim	30/06/1919	30/06/1919
War Diary	Bedburg	01/07/1919	07/07/1919
War Diary	Hilden	08/07/1919	31/08/1919
War Diary	Hilden	02/09/1919	02/09/1919
War Diary	Hilden	01/09/1919	02/11/1919

No 25/13/14) 10

2 ~~LIGHT~~ (2) DIVISION

3 LIGHT BRIGADE

51 BN. RIFLE BRIGADE

1919 MAR – 1919 OCT

3rd Bn Rifle Brigade

WAR DIARY
INTELLIGENCE SUMMARY

Army Form C. 2118.

for March 1919.
1 April

Place	Date	Hour	Summary of Events and Information	Remarks and references to Appendices
STOMMELN	26.3.19	17.20	The Battalion left COLCHESTER on the morning of the 21st. Embarked at DOVER 1300 same day, arriving DUNKERQUE at 1600. Here the night was spent out at 1400 next day proceeded by train arriving STOMMELN, GERMANY, 0600 on the 24th. Billets were taken over there from 1st K.R.R.C. On the 25th "C" Coy moved to Billets in FLIESTEDEN and the Transport was taken over from the 24th R. Fusiliers and was billeted at INGENDORF. On the 26.3.19 Capt A.C. HEPBURN, R.A.M.C. (T) returned to ENGLAND and Capt J.D BATT. A.C. R.A.M.C joined the Bn. as M.O.	maps. ref: GERMANY 1L & 1K SCALE 1/100,000.
STOMMELN	31.3.19	17.00	Brig-General R.A.A. CURRIE C.M.G. D.S.O visited the Battalion & inspected billets. 13 men attached to 99 F. French Mortar Batty. at MONCHOF FARM, RHEIDT.	

B. Porter
Major
Commanding
3rd Bn Rifle Brigade

Conf^d. Army Form C. 2118.

WAR DIARY
or
INTELLIGENCE SUMMARY.
(Erase heading not required.)

Instructions regarding War Diaries and Intelligence Summaries are contained in F.S. Regs., Part II. and the Staff Manual respectively. Title pages will be prepared in manuscript.

Place	Date	Hour	Summary of Events and Information	Remarks and references to Appendices
STOMMELN	1.4.19	17.30	Usual Training carried out.	
-do-	2.4.19	17.00	—do—	
-do-	3.4.19	17.20	Lt. Gen. Sir A.J. GODLEY, K.C.B., K.C.M.G. visited the Battalion, inspected billets and the B^n at training. Three Platoons, one from each Coy A, B & D, proceeded to COLOGNE to be attached to 17th Lan.cers. The former a composite company under the command of Capt. P.J.L. CHARRINGTON. M.C. The Lan.cers train were A Coy, 2/Lt W.E. LEA, B Coy, Lt. J.H.F. JOHNSTON, D Coy 2nd Lt W. WALES.	
-do-	4.4.19	17.00	Usual Training carried out.	
-do-	5.4.19	17.00	—do—	
-do-	6.4.19	17.00	Brig. Gen. R.A.H. CURRIE. C.M.G. D.S.O. attended Church Parade.	
-do-	7.4.19	17.00	Billeting party proceeded to BEDBURG.	
BEDBURG	8.4.19	17.20	The B^n moved to BEDBURG by road, leaving STOMMELN 0830 hrs arriving BEDBURG 1215 hrs. Billeted in North end of the Town. The "R" becomes 1/the 3rd Polish Brigade, commanded by Brig-Genl. H.B.P.L. KENNEDY, the other Bns. of the Bde being the 52nd & 53rd B^ns the Rifle Brigade.	Route:- ROMMERSKIRCHEN –HUSHELHOVEN– FRAUWEILER– BEDBURG.
-do-	9.4.19	17.00	Lt-Col G.H. LIDDELL. D.S.O. joined the Battalion.	
-do-	10.4.19	17.25	Major E.B. POWELL proceeded to MEDENAUSSEM to take command of the 9th B^n London.	

57th Bn. The Rifle Brigade

WAR DIARY or INTELLIGENCE SUMMARY

April 1919

Army Form C. 2118.

Place	Date	Hour	Summary of Events and Information	Remarks and references to Appendices
BEDBURG	11.4.19	17:15	Regt. M. Col. G.W. LIDDELL, D.S.O. takes over command of the Battalion	
-do-	11.4.19	18:30	Usual Training carried out.	
-do-	12.4.19	18:30	Usual Training carried out. 2nd Lt. F.G. Parry (Worcestershire Regt) and W.F.C. BROOKSBANK proceed home to ENGLAND, being Regular Officers, in accordance with A.G. 8658 (O) of 30.3.19.	
-do-	13.4.19	18:00	2nd A.M. GARROOD & 2nd A.W. McCRORIE proceed to ENGLAND to be demobilized.	
-do-	14.4.19	18:00	Brig. Gen. H.R.B.L. KENNEDY Commanding 3rd Light Brigade inspected the Bn on Parade. Lt. F.C. Davenport. A Coy demob'd 13 Ech.	
-do-	15.4.19	18:00	Usual Training carried out.	
-do-	16.4.19	16:30	Usual Training carried out. Capt. R.A.C. FOSTER (O.C. D Coy) demob'd 13 Ech.	
-do-	17.4.19	18:00	Usual Training carried out. 2nd Lt. W.H. Taggart takes command of "D" Coy.	
-do-	18.4.19	18:00	Good Friday. Capt. P.R.L. Charrington demobilized.	
-do-	19.4.19	18:00	"C" Coy moves from BUCHOLZ & LIPP into R. of BEDBURG.	
-do-	20.4.19	18:30	Easter Sunday.	
-do-	21.4.19	18:00	Easter Monday whole holiday.	
-do-	22.4.19	18:30	Usual Training carried out.	PSC

57th Bn The Rifle Brigade

WAR DIARY April 1919.

Army Form C. 2118.

INTELLIGENCE SUMMARY.

(Erase heading not required.)

Instructions regarding War Diaries and Intelligence Summaries are contained in F. S. Regs., Part II. and the Staff Manual respectively. Title pages will be prepared in manuscript.

Place	Date	Hour	Summary of Events and Information	Remarks and references to Appendices
BEDBURG	23.4.19	18.00	Usual Training. Carried out.	
-do-	24.4.19	18.00	13 men & 1 sub/Lt detailed to form 3rd Light Bde Trench Mortar Batty at MILLENDORF. 2nd Lt C.W. Stokes proceeds to ENGLAND for course of Education at NEWMARKET. Lt Denton & 2 Lt H. Finch joined the B".	
-do-	25.4.19	18.00	Usual Training carried out. Capt. RE Castle R.C. RAMC attached to the B" takes the place of Capt-Batt who goes on leave. Capt. R.I.P. Humphry (O.C. B Coy) proceeded home to England. Lieut B.A. Horne takes over the command of "B" Coy. Lt Denton takes over the command "D's" Coy.	
-do-	26.4.19	18.30	2nd Lt M.H. Peacock returns to England. Relieving officer returns to Bn. B" Coy moves from BROTCH into SUGAR FACTORY at North end of BEDBURG. K.R.R.C.	
-do-	27.4.19	18.00	Lt Col C.H.W. Seymour D.S.O takes over command of the "B"" from Lt Col Lidwell who becomes 2nd in command.	
-do-	28.4.19	17.00	Usual Training carried out.	
-do-	29.4.19	18.30	Usual Training carried out.	
-do-	30.4.19	17.00	250 Htn Ammunition issued to officers.	

ASeymour
Lieut Col
2/5/19 57th Battn The Rifle Brigade

Army Form C. 2118.

WAR DIARY
or
INTELLIGENCE SUMMARY.

(Erase heading not required.)

51st Bn THE RIFLE BRIGADE

MAY 1919

Instructions regarding War Diaries and Intelligence Summaries are contained in F.S. Regs., Part II. and the Staff Manual respectively. Title pages will be prepared in manuscript.

Place	Date	Hour	Summary of Events and Information	Remarks and references to Appendices
BEDBURG	1/5/19	18.00	2nd Lieut. W.P.S. CURTIS proceeded to ENGLAND (being regular Officer) to report to Depot. †	Authority a.g. 8658(0) † 30.3.19
- do -	2/5/19	18.00	Usual training carried out. Divisional Education Officer visited Battalion. Major General Sir R.D. WHIGHAM KCB DSO inspected the Battn at 10.00 hours at SCHLOSS.	
- do -	3/5/19	18.00	Usual training carried out	
- do -	4/5/19	18.30	SUNDAY.	
- do -	5/5/19	18.30	Usual training carried out.	
- do -	6/5/19	19.30	H.R.H. Field Marshal The Duke of Connaught (Colonel in Chief of the Rifle Brigade) inspected the Battn at 16.00, on Football Ground at Eastern end of village. The Battn afterwards marched past in Column of Route.	
- do -	7/5/19		Captn J.H. LEE. D.S.O. proceeded to join 20th Bn KRRC. ZONS. One other rank Demobilized	
- do -	8/5/19	17.50	Usual training carried out.	
- do -	9/5/19	18.30	Major G.W. LIDDELL D.S.O. proceeded to join 53rd RIFLE BRIGADE, BEDBURG. Major The Hon. N.C. GATHORNE HARDY, D.S.O. joined the Bn from 53rd RIFLE BRIG. as 2nd in command vice Major G.W. LIDDELL. DSO. Lieut N.C. DENTON on leave.	
- do -	10/5/19	18.00	Usual training carried out	
	11/5/19		SUNDAY	

T2134. Wt. W708—776. 500000. 4/15. Sir J.C. & S.

5⁰ᵗ Bⁿ The RIFLE BRIGADE

Army Form C. 2118.

WAR DIARY or INTELLIGENCE SUMMARY

(Erase heading not required.)

MAY 1919

Place	Date	Hour	Summary of Events and Information	Remarks and references to Appendices
BEDBURG	12/5/19	19.00	Usual training carried out.	
- do -	13/5/19	19.00	Usual training carried out.	
- do -	14/5/19	19.30	12 other ranks demobilized. Usual training carried out.	
- do -	15/5/19	18.30	Usual training carried out. One other rank demobilized.	
- do -	16/5/19	19.00	Bⁿ route march.	
- do -	17/5/19	18.00	Usual training carried out.	
- do -	18/5/19	19.00	SUNDAY.	
- do -	19/5/19	18.30	CAPTN. J.D. BATT. M.C. R.A.M.C. (medical Officer) rejoins from leave, and resumes duties of medical Officer vice CAPTN CARTER M.C. who goes to 6ᵗʰ Field Ambulance.	
- do -	20/5/19	19.00	Usual training carried out.	
- do -	21/5/19	19.00	Lt GOULD M.C. and Lt G.L. RUMBLE demobilized. Also 2 other ranks.	
- do -	22/5/19	17.00	Usual training carried out.	
- do -	23/5/19	14.30	Battalion route march, men cooked their own dinners whilst out.	
- do -	24/5/19	18.00	Empire Day observed as a holiday. LT N.C. DENTON rejoins from leave to U.K.	
- do -	25/5/19	16.30	SUNDAY.	
- do -	26/5/19	18.30	Usual training carried out.	

WAR DIARY
or
INTELLIGENCE SUMMARY.
(Erase heading not required.)

Army Form C. 2118.

57 Bn. The Rifle Brigade

May 1919

Place	Date	Hour	Summary of Events and Information	Remarks and references to Appendices
BEDBURG	27 5/19	19.00	Usual training carried out.	
- do -	28 5/19	17.00	Major H.E.F. SICH demobilized and 1 other rank. Usual training carried out.	
- do -	29 5/19	16.00	The Commander-in-chief inspected the Battn. with the 53rd Rifle Bde at 0945 on the Football Field. Battalion paraded 523 o.r. strength in Fighting order, in Mass, Transport in rear. The Battalion afterwards marched past the Commander-in-chief in column of route.	
- do -	30 5/19	16.00	Battalion Route marched from 0800 - 1130. The Divisional Comdr. inspected cooking arrangements of B Company only.	
- do -	31 5/19	19.00	Interior Economy and Training carried out. Serjeants' Rifle Meeting.	

N. Falzine Green
Major
Comdg. 51st Bn, The Rifle Bde.

WAR DIARY

Army Form C. 2118.

5th Batln The Rifle Brigade

INTELLIGENCE SUMMARY

June 1919

(Erase heading not required.)

Instructions regarding War Diaries and Intelligence Summaries are contained in F.S. Regs., Part II. and the Staff Manual respectively. Title Pages will be prepared in manuscript.

Place	Date	Hour	Summary of Events and Information	Remarks and references to Appendices
Bedburg	1	1400	Brigade Church Parade	
	2	2100	Usual Training carried out.	
	3	2100	Birthday of H.M. the King. Brigade Paraded at 1000 for Royal Salute and Three Cheers. Reminder of the day observed as Royal Holiday. Company Sports or Rifle Meeting in the afternoon. Comdg Officer proceeds on	
	4	1700	6 Sergeants sent to disposal.	
			short leave.	
	5	2200	Usual Training carried out.	
	6	2230	Route-march postponed owing to bad weather.	
	7	1001	Usual Training.	
	8	1400	Brigade Church service in Y.M.C.A. Battalion Sports in afternoon	
	9	1500	Whit Monday. No Training carried out. Recreation by Coys etc	
	10	2100	Usual Training.	
	11	2000	Battalion Rifle Meeting. Inter-coy aggregate Challenge Cup R.Q.M.S. Schumacks gym Green & 3 Sgts and 2/cos demobilized.	
	12	2130	Battalion Rifle Meeting. Individual and Team Events.	
	13	2130	Route March – Starting at 0600 hours	
	14	2045	5 Reenlisted men sent for dispersal.	
	15	1400	Brigade Church Parade 1100 hours. Divisional Commander, Maj. Gen. Jeffreys, attended	

5th Battn
The Rifle Brigade

WAR DIARY
INTELLIGENCE SUMMARY
(Erase heading not required.)

Army Form C. 2118.

Place	Date	Hour	Summary of Events and Information	Remarks and references to Appendices
Bedburg	June 16 17	1900	Usual Training carried out. Received warning to move on the 18th en route for Cologne Area. Orders issued to concentrating and loading Transport.	
GIESSEN	18	2200	Moved from Bedburg starting at 0720 and marching via BERGHEIM - NIEDERAUSSEM. H.Q., A & B companies to GIESSEN. C & D companies to FLIESTEDEN. Major-Gen. JEFFERYS inspected the Battn. in Column on route outside NIEDERAUSSEM. Arrived in good billets about 1130. Orders issued for resumption of march to EHRENFELD on the 19th. Moving in Fighting order	
CÖLN - NIPPES	19	2200	Marched via BRAUWEILER - WIDDERSDORF - BOCKLEMUND - BICKENDORF to NIPPES finding on allotted billets at PIUS ST. SCHOOLS still occupied by 6th London, after waiting for 30 minutes in EHRENFELD occupied billets in NIPPES. H.Q. A & B companies in School HARTWICH STR., C & D companies in School OSSENDORFER STR. which was still partly occupied by a rear party of the 1/4 YORK & LANCASTER Regt.	
–	20	1700	Battalion stands to in NIPPES, orders to relief of Guards turned by 1st London Bde. issued. 350 N.C.O.s and men required.	

5st Battn
The Rifle Brigade

WAR DIARY
INTELLIGENCE SUMMARY
Army Form C. 2118.

Place	Date	Hour	Summary of Events and Information	Remarks and references to Appendices
COLN - NIPPES	21	2100	Battalion All standing by. Move across the Rhine postponed.	
"	22	1400	Sunday.	
"	23	1700	Usual Training carried out.	
"	24	1700	Usual Training carried out.	
"	25	2100	Usual Training carried out. Lieut Gen. Haldane comdg VI Corps visited the Battalion. ERMS Cole proceeded to demobilisation	
"	26	22.00	Usual Training carried out.	
"	27	23.00	Usual Training carried out	
"	28	1415	Usual Training carried out. Battalion Drill at 1000. C.O. addresses the Battn. after parade. Peace Treaty was signed at 1500 hours. Orders received to return to normal area.	
"	29	2145		
Poulheim	30	2000	Battalion moved by march route from NIPPES and billetted for the night in buildings at Poulheim. started at 0630 and arrived at 0915. Advanced party proceeded at 1700 to Bedburg.	

Bedburg 2/7/19

Wyman Lieut. Col.
commanding
5th Battn The Rifle Rfle

51st Bn. The Rifle Brigade.

WAR DIARY
or
INTELLIGENCE SUMMARY.
(Erase heading not required.)

Instructions regarding War Diaries and Intelligence Summaries are contained in F.S. Regs., Part II. and the Staff Manual respectively. Title pages will be prepared in manuscript.

Army Form C. 2118.

JULY 1919

Place	Date	Hour	Summary of Events and Information	Remarks and references to Appendices
BEDBURG.	July. 1st.	2200	Bn. Moved to BEDBURG via STOMMELN, RHEIDT, and FRAUWEILER, starting at 0500. Weather good. Arrived at BEDBURG at 0900. "C" & "D" Companies occupied camp at foot of BUCHOLZ hill and "B" the Sugar Factory, and "A" the East end of the town, with one Platoon in Camp. The SCHLOSS is occupied by R.A.M.C. Transport returned to Sugar Factory. Major the Hon GATHORNE HARDY rejoined from leave to U.K.	
--:---	2nd	1900	Usual training carried out.	
--:---	3rd	1800	--:---	
--:---	4th	2000	CAPTAIN W. CHESTER on leave to U.K. Usual training carried out.	
--:---	5th	1800	Usual training carried out.	
--:---	6th	1800	SUNDAY.	
--:---	7th	1700	Usual training carried out.	
HILDEN	8th	2000	Bn. moved to HILDEN by train via COLOGNE, starting at 1100, weather dull. Arrived HILDEN 1600 less 3 outposts in billets in HILDEN. 2/Lt. A.E. BOYLAND and 40 other ranks at No. 1 Outpost at KEMPERDICK. 2/Lt. S. RAINGES and 25 other ranks at No. 2 Outpost DICKHAUS. Lt. P.E.V. Goodson and 40 other ranks at RHEINSHOLZ at No. 3 Outpost.	
--:---	9th	2100	Bn. settled in at HILDEN. Outposts visited. Lt. G. HANNAM joins Lt. GOODSON at No. 3 Outpost and takes over Command.	
--:---	10th	2200	Usual training carried out.	
--:---	11th	2100	Bn. Drill 1000 until 1100.	

Army Form C. 2118.

5[1]st Battn. Rifle Brigade,　　　Sheet 2.

WAR DIARY
or
~~INTELLIGENCE SUMMARY.~~
(Erase heading not required.)

July 1919.

Instructions regarding War Diaries and Intelligence Summaries are contained in F.S. Regs., Part II. and the Staff Manual respectively. Title pages will be prepared in manuscript.

Place	Date	Hour	Summary of Events and Information	Remarks and references to Appendices
HILDEN.	July. 12th	1800	R.S.M. Hawthorn joins for duty. 2/Lt. P. Romney proceeded to Dickhaus outpost with one Platoon and relieves 2/Lt. D.S. HAINGES and one Platoon.	
---:---	13th	2200	SUNDAY.	
---:---	14th	1700	Usual training carried out	
---:---	15th	1800	2/Lt. G.A.M. GOODFELLOW relieves 2/Lt. BOYLAND at KEMPERDICK Post. Lt. De PASS, relieves Lieut. P.E.V. GOODSON at REISHOLZ Post (Some shots fired at REISHOLZ Post, - no casualties.)	
---:---	16th	1730	"D" Company fires on Ranges. 2/Lt. BOYLAND and 15 other ranks demobilized. Lieut. B.M. Steger rejoins from leave to U.K.	
---:---	17th	1900	"D" Company fires on Ranges.	
---:---	18th	1800	2/Lt. RAMBERT goes on leave to U.K. Some shots fired at DICKHAUS POST. 2 Germans wounded.	
---:---	19th	1900	Captain BATT, M.C. goes on leave. DICKHAUS and KEMPERDICK Garrisons relieved, by "B" Company.	
---:---	20th	1700	SUNDAY. REISHOLZ Garrison relieved by "D" Company. Captain CHESTER rejoins from leave	
---:---	21st	2200	2/Lt. L.A. CEAL goes on leave to U.K.	
---:---	22nd	1800	"C" Company firing on range. Very wet.	
---:---	23rd	1600	Observed as PEACE HOLIDAY. SPORTS cancelled owing to rain. Captain. R. BRICKWOOD DSO joins Battalion from England.	

Army Form C. 2118.

51st Battn. Rifle Brigade. Sheet. 3.

WAR DIARY
or
INTELLIGENCE SUMMARY

July 1919.

(Erase heading not required.)

Instructions regarding War Diaries and Intelligence Summaries are contained in F. S. Regs., Part II. and the Staff Manual respectively. Title pages will be prepared in manuscript.

Place	Date	Hour	Summary of Events and Information	Remarks and references to Appendices
HILDEN.	24th	2200	Usual training carried out.	
--------	25th	1800	Usual training carried out.	
--------	26th	1600	Lieut. J.H.S. JOHNSTON goes on leave to U.K. 2/Lt. KITCHEN joins for duty. Posted to "D" Coy.	
--------	27th	1900	SUNDAY. "A" & "C" Companies commence firing G.M.C. Weather dull and wet.	
--------	28th	1800	G.M.C. continued; weather still wet and dull. Brig. General H.B. KENNEDY C.M.G., D.S.O. inspected Battalion Billets.	
--------	29th	2100	"A" & "C" Companies continue G.M.C. Weather still dull	
--------	30th	2100	"A" & "C" Companies continue G.M.C. Weather still dull.	
--------	31st	1900	2/Lt. W. WALES proceeded on leave to U.K. "A" & "C" Coys continue G.M.C. weather dull	

HILDEN.
2-8-1919.

J.F. Johnstone Major
Lieut.-Colonel,
Commanding,
51st Battalion The Rifle Brigade.

Army Form C.2118.

WAR DIARY
or
INTELLIGENCE SUMMARY

(Erase heading not required.)

51st Battalion, The Rifle Brigade.

AUGUST, 1919.

Instructions regarding War Diaries and Intelligence Summaries are contained in F.S. Regs., Part II. and the Staff Manual respectively. Title Pages will be prepared in manuscript.

Place	Date	Hour	Summary of Events and Information	Remarks and references to Appendices
HILDEN.	1/8/19	1800	"A" and "C" Companies fire G.M.C. weather dull and windy.	
-do-	2/8/19	2100	Lieut. W.H.Taggart goes on leave to U.K. "A" Company on Range.	
-do-	3/8/19	1600	SUNDAY.	
-do-	4/8/19	1900	Transport Show at Cologne. "A" and "C" Companies relieve "B" and "D" Companies on the Outposts 2nd/Lieut. G.H.Lambert rejoins from leave to U.K.	
-do-	5/8/19	2100	"B" and "D" Companies begin firing their G.M.C. weather dull. Lieut. G.H.Mercer on leave to U.K. "A" Company evacuate MEIDE and go into same building as "C" and "D" companies.	
-do-	6/8/19	1800	Capt. W.W.Brown on leave to U.K. "B" and "D" Companies continue G.M.C. in dull weather.	
-do-	7/8/19	1800	"B" and "D" Companies continue G.M.C. weather alternatly bright and dull.	
-do-	8/8/19	2130	Lieut. H.P.Parker and Capt. B.A.Fixsen on leave to U.K. G.M.C. continued by "B" and "D" Companies. Maj.-Gen. G.D.Jeffreys CB., C.M.G. inspected billets of the Battalion. 2nd/Lieut. L.A.Ceal rejoined from leave to U.K.	Major R.Brickwo takes ov and in Co 6/8/19.
-do-	9/8/19	2200	"B" and "D" Companies continue G.M.C. weather alternately bright and cloudy. 2nd/Lieut. L.A Ceal joins REISHOLZ Control Post for duty with Station Control.	Ceal-Gathorne-Hardy, D. proceeds to Engl. to report to Depot Capt.
-do-	10/8/19	1800	"B" and "D" Companies continue G.M.C. weather very bright.	
-do-	11/8/19	1800	Capt. E.D.Lindow, Medical Officer, on leave to U.K. Medical Officer of 52nd Battn. acting as Medical Officer i/c Battalion. "D" Company continue G.M.C. Lieut. J.H.S.Johnston rejoined from leave to U.K.	
-do-	12/8/19	1730	Lieut. J.Lamont on leave to U.K. 1 Officer and 50 Other Ranks commenced barbed wire entanglements in advanced section of perimeter of zone of occupation.	
-do-	13/8/19	1800	1 Officer and 50 Other Ranks continued work on the barbed wire entanglements.	
-do-	14/8/19	1730	Brigadier General H.B.Kennedy,C.M.G.,D.S.O. inspected the villets and Dining Halls of the Battalion. 1 Officer and 50 Other Ranks continued work on the barbed wire entanglements.	
-do-	15/8/19	1800	1 Officer and 50 Other Ranks continued work on the barbed wire entanglements.	
-do-	16/8/19	1815	1 Officer and 50 Other Ranks continued work on the barbed wire entanglements.	
-do-	17/8/19	1715	SUNDAY. 2nd/Lieut. W.Wales rejoined from leave to U.K.	
-do-	18/8/19	1900	One Officer and 50 Other Ranks completed work on the barbed wire entanglements. Lieut. W.H.Taggart rejoined from leave to U.K. Btn. Transport 4th prize at Rhine Army Horse Show.	
-do-	19/8/19	1830	"B" and "D" relieved "A" and "C" Companies at the Outposts. Lieut Membrey and Lieut de Pass proceeded to U.K. on leave.	
-do-	20/8/19	1845	Usual training carried out.	

Army Form C. 2118.

WAR DIARY
or
INTELLIGENCE SUMMARY

51st Battalion. The Rifle Brigade.

(Erase heading not required.)

Instructions regarding War Diaries and Intelligence Summaries are contained in F. S. Regs., Part II. and the Staff Manual respectively. Title Pages AUGUST, 1919. will be prepared in manuscript.

Place	Date	Hour	Summary of Events and Information	Remarks and references to Appendices
HILDEN	21/8/19	1930	Lieuts. W.E.Lea and D.S.Fainges proceeded on leave to U.K. Major G.W.Liddell,D.S.O. took over command of the Battalion from Lt.-Col. C.H.N.Seymour,D.S.O. First day of Brigade Sports.	
-do-	22/8/19	1915	Capt. M.W.Brown rejoined from leave U.K. Second day of Brigade Sports. Capt.(T/Major) G.W.Liddell, D.S.O. appointed acting Lt.-Col. whilst in command of the Battalion.	
-do-	23/8/19	1900	Usual training carried out.	
-do-	24/8/19	1800	Usual training carried out. Capt. B.A.Fixsen rejoins from U.K. leave.	
-do-	25/8/19	1930	Regimental Brithday Sports. Holiday granted. Weather fine. Lieut, H.P.Parker rejoins from U.K. leave. Lieut. E.Kitching and Lieut. C.W.Stokes on leave to U.K.	
-do-	26/8/19	2000	Capt. C.W.Tait,M.C. rejoins from U.K. leave.	
-do-	27/8/19	1800	Lieut. B.A.Morrow on leave to U.K. Usual training carried out.	
-do-	28/8/19	1900	Usual training carried out. Lieut. J.Lamont rejoins from U.K. Leave.	
-do-	29/8/19	2100	Usual training carried out.	
-do-	30/8/19	2130	Usual training carried out.	
-do-	31/8/19	1600	SUNDAY.	

HILDEN.
2/9/19.

[signature] Lt.-Col.
Commanding,
51st Battalion The Rifle Brigade.

Army Form C. 2118.

WAR DIARY
or
INTELLIGENCE SUMMARY
(Erase heading not required.)

51st Battalion, THE RIFLE BRIGADE.

SEPTEMBER, 1919.

Instructions regarding War Diaries and Intelligence Summaries are contained in F. S. Regs., Part II. and the Staff Manual respectively. Title Pages will be prepared in manuscript.

Place	Date	Hour	Summary of Events and Information	Remarks and references to Appendices
HILDEN.	1/9/19	1900	"C" & "D" Companies relieve "A" and "B" on outpost duties. 2/Lieut. G.A.M.Goodfellow demobilized.	
do	2/9/19	2100	Usual training carried out. 1 O.S.M. and 1 sergeant joined for duty. Lieut. B.M.Steger transferred to Rifle Brigade from Royal West Surrey Regiment.	
do	3/9/19	1700	Usual training carried out.	
do	4/9/19	1900	Light Divisional Sports, weather fine and warm. Lieut D.H. de Pass and Lieut. R.H.Membrey rejoined from U.K. leave.	
do	5/9/19	2000	Usual training carried out.	
do	6/9/19	1600	3 other ranks proceed to Cologne for demobilization. Lieut. W.E.Lea rejoined from U.K. leave.	
do	7/9/19	1800	3 othe ranks proceed to Cologne for demobilization. - SUNDAY - Lieut. G. Hannan rejoined from U.K. leave.	
do	8/9/19	2000	Major-General G. D. JEFFREYS,C.B.,C.M.G. inspected the Battalion less "A" and "C" Companies. 3 other ranks demobilized. Capt. E.S.Barraclough,M.G. joined for duty from 53rd Rifle Bde. Lieut. P.E.V.Goodson goes on leave to U.K.leave. 3other rank demobilized. Capt. E.S.Barraclough,M.G. takes over command of "D" Company from Lieut. W.H.Taggart. Capt.M.W.Brown transferred to Rifle	
do	9/9/19	1500	Brigade from South Wales Borderers. 3 other ranks demobilized. Lieut. W.Wales to Hospital. Lieut. G.W.Stokes rejoins from U.K. leave.	
do	10/9/19	1800	Usual training carried out.	
do	11/9/19	1900	Lieut.B.A.Morrow rejoins from U.K. leave. Usual training carried out.	
do	12/9/19	1700	Usual training carried out.	
do	13/9/19	1800	SUNDAY. Lieut. E.Kitching rejoined from U.K.leave.	
do	14/9/19	1600	Lieut.M.C.Denton goes on U.K. leave. Outposts relieved in order to start firing Lewis Gun Course and casuals of the Battalion to fire G.M.G.	
do	15/9/19	1800		
do	16/9/19	1900	2 other ranks demobilized. Lewis Gunners and casuals on Range.	
do	17/9/19	1800	5 other ranks demobilized. Lewis Gunners and casuals on Range.S	
do	18/9/19	1800	15 other ranks demobilized. Lewis Gunners and casuals on Range. Capt. M.W.Brown 4 days leave to U.K. Lieut. G.E.Burton goes on leave to U.K.	
do	19/9/19	1700	13 other ranks demobilized. LewisGunners and casuals on Range.	
do	20/9/19	1800	34 other ranks demobilized. Lewis Gunners and casuals on Range. Lieut. B.M.Steger proceeded on leave to U.K.	
do	21/9/19	1600	SUNDAY. Lewis Gunners and casuals on Range.	
do	22/9/19	1730	Lewis Gunners on Range. 2nd/Lieut.P.Romney proceeded on leave to U.K.	

Sheet 2.

Army Form C. 2118.

WAR DIARY
or
INTELLIGENCE SUMMARY

51st Battalion, THE RIFLE BRIGADE.

SEPTEMBER, 1919.

(Erase heading not required.)

Instructions regarding War Diaries and Intelligence Summaries are contained in F.S. Regs, Part II. and the Staff Manual respectively. Title Pages will be prepared in manuscript.

Place	Date	Hour	Summary of Events and Information	Remarks and references to Appendices
HILDEN.	23/9/19	1800	Usual training carried out.	
do	24/9/19	1730	"D" Company relieve "B" Company at the Outposts. Capt. M.W.Brown rejoined from leave to U.K.	
do	25/9/19	1730	Strike in progress in Coppel's Factory,Hilden. The Battalion made a raid during the night of 24/25 and apprehended 10 strike leaders who were despatched under escort to Cologne.	
do	26/9/19	1730	Usual training carried out. Lieut. P.E.V.Goodson rejoined from U.K. leave. An additional strike leader apprehended during the night of 25/26. KELLERTHOR Outpost taken over by the Battalion from 12th Royal Irish Rifles and Garrisoned by "B" Company. One platoon from "C" Company proceeded to Ohligs to furnish Divisional Commander's Guard. 6 Officers and 15 other ranks attended a lecture given by Sir George Paish at the Divisional College, Ohligs.	
do	27/9/19	1800	As usual.	
do	28/9/19	1600	SUNDAY.	
do	29/9/19	1730	As usual.	
do	30/9/19	1800	As usual.	

HILDEN.

1st October,1919.

E.W.... Lieutenant-Colonel,
Commanding,
51st Battalion, The Rifle Brigade.

Army Form C. 2118.

WAR DIARY
or
INTELLIGENCE SUMMARY

(Erase heading not required.)

OCTOBER, 1919.

1st Battalion, The Rifle Brigade.

Instructions regarding War Diaries and Intelligence Summaries are contained in F. S. Regs., Part II. and the Staff Manual respectively. Title Pages will be prepared in manuscript.

Place	Date	Hour	Summary of Events and Information	Remarks and references to Appendices
HILDEN	1/10/19	1700	As usual.	
do	2/10/19	1800	"C" Company by "A" at Reisholz Outpost.	
do	3/10/19	1630	As usual.	
do	4/10/19	1815	As usual.	
do	5/10/19	1600	SUNDAY.	
do	6/10/19	1700	Training as usual.	
do	7/10/19	1700	Lieuts. Hannam and de Pass with 15 other ranks take over control of Hilden Station. One platoon of "C" Company returned from Ohligs after having performed the duties of Divisional Commander's Guard.	
do	8/10/19	1800	As usual.	
do	9/10/19	1700	Lieut. P. Romney rejoined from leave to U.K. Training as usual.	
do	10/10/19	1800	As usual.	
do	11/10/19	1800	As usual.	
do	12/10/19	1630	SUNDAY. 5 other ranks demobilized.	
do	13/10/19	1700	Advanced billetting party sent to Schlebusch. One French Officer and two men arrive as advanced party to take over.	
do	14/10/19	1700	Move cancelled. 4 other ranks demobilized.	
do	15/10/19	1800	Major Brickwood proceeded on leave to U.K.	
do	16/10/19	1730	The advanced billeting party rejoined battalion from Schlebusch. 5 other ranks demobilized.	
do	17/10/19	1730	14 other ranks demobilized.	
do	18/10/19	1945	Lieut. N.C. Denton rejoins from leave to U.K.	
do	19/10/19	1730	SUNDAY.	
do	20/10/19	1800	As usual.	
do	21/10/19	1700	Lieut. C.G. Piper, 2/Lt. W.T. Goodwin, D.C.M. and A.E. Bowler, 1 C.S.M. and 85 other ranks joined the battalion having been transferred from the 53rd Battn., The Rifle Brigade.	
do	22/10/19	1800	2/Lt. N.M. McRobert joins the battalion from the 3rd Rifle Bde. Capt. W. Chester proceeded on leave to U.K.	
do	23/10/19	1800	2/Lt. A.E. Bower proceeded on leave to U.K. Capt. E.S. Barraclough, M.C., Lieut. J. Lamont, Lieut. G. Hannam, 2/Lieut. P. Romney and 5 other ranks proceeded to Cologne for dispersal.	
do	24/10/19	1700	Lieuts. Taggart, Goodson and kitching proceeded to Cologne for dispersal.	
do	25/10/19	1800	Capt. J. Morris, Lieuts. H.M. Abercrombie and D. McCaffrey and 2/Lt. B.A. McShane join Battalion from Detachment at Bniuge Reception Camp, Cologne. One other rank proceeded for dispersal.	

Sheet 2.

Army Form C. 2118.

WAR DIARY
or
INTELLIGENCE SUMMARY

OCTOBER, 1919.

51st Battalion, The Rifle Bde.

(Erase heading not required.)

Instructions regarding War Diaries and Intelligence Summaries are contained in F. S. Regs., Part II. and the Staff Manual respectively. Title Pages will be prepared in manuscript.

Place	Date	Hour	Summary of Events and Information	Remarks and references to Appendices
Hilden.	26/10/19	1730	SUNDAY. Lieut. B.W.Hall, M.C. joined Battalion from leave to U.K. having been transferred from 53rd Bn. The Rifle Bde.	
do	27/10/19	1730	One other rank proceeded for dispersal.	
do	28/10/19	1800	Capt. R. Holland, Lieut. J.D.Davidson, M.C. and 118 other ranks joined the battalion from the RhineArmy Concentration Camp, Cologne having been transferred from 53rd Bn. The Rifle Brigade. Lieut. B.M.Steger and 2/Lt. G.E.Burton rejoined from leave to U.K.	
do	29/10/19	1900	Lieut. Read joined Battalionfrom Reisholz Station Control. 2/Lt. G.R.Boyd taken on strength from 53rd Battalion; from 22/10/19.	
do	30/10/19	1700	Usual training carried out. Lt.-Col. the Hon R.Brand, C.M.G., D.S.O. assumes command of the Battalion vice Lt.-Col. G.W.Liddell, D.S.O. who becomesSSecond in Command vice Major R.Brickwood, D.S.O.	
do	31/10/19	1900	Lieut. H.P.Parker and Lieut. D.H.de Pass demobilized.	

HILDEN.
2/11/19.

R. Brand
Lieut.-Colonel,
Commanding,
51st Battalion, The Rifle Brigade.

www.ingramcontent.com/pod-product-compliance
Lightning Source LLC
Chambersburg PA
CBHW081508160426
43193CB00014B/2620